T0128699

Which Church Are You?

<hr>

Are You Real or Just Going Through the Motions?

Dr. Darrow Perkins, Jr., Th.D.

authorHOUSE®

AuthorHouse™
1663 Liberty Drive
Bloomington, IN 47403
www.authorhouse.com
Phone: 1 (800) 839-8640

Published by AuthorHouse 01/13/2017

ISBN: 978-1-5246-5592-1 (sc)
ISBN: 978-1-5246-5591-4 (hc)
ISBN: 978-1-5246-5593-8 (e)

Library of Congress Control Number: 2016921125

Print information available on the last page.

DEDICATION

This book is dedicated to my father, Darrow Perkins, Sr., (1940-2016) whom I loved dearly and in his own way, taught me many things about life, living, and the importance of having a relationship with Jesus Christ.

INTRODUCTION

Church today is nothing like it was when I was growing up in Baton Rouge and New Orleans, LA during the 70's and 80's, and I understand that as times change, things change. One of the biggest changes that the church has gone through is the lack of commitment to its given mandate and ministries. There are so many distractions today that people tend to work God into their personal schedules, instead of working their schedules around God and His ministry.

Another thing I've noticed is that the "church," although it has changed over time, is very similar to the churches in which Jesus was addressing in the Book of Revelation, Chapters 2 & 3. Having had the opportunity to travel across the United States and internationally, I have found that the various churches I've visited and attended fall into one of the seven churches of Asia Minor that Jesus was dealing with. The Lord, knowing how He wants His church to function and look like, was in the best position possible to identify their strengths and weaknesses. Once we come to grips with the reality that we're not perfect and we have room for improvement, we can then begin to take the steps necessary to be the best church possible for the Lord and His kingdom. But I've found out that it's not the church organization that needs improvement, it's what I call the "individual church." It's the individual member that makes up the church, and the Lord was identifying some of the traits, characteristics, and imperfections of the church...meaning within the members!

I have learned that the first step to solving a problem is to identify it, and the goal of this book is to share what was identified as wrong, so the "individual church" can make the adjustments to be right before the Lord. It is my sincere prayer that these few words of insight will be a benefit to you and your Christian journey! Blessings...

Serving the Lord and His People,

Dr. Darrow Perkins, Jr.

CONTENTS

Chapter 1

The Church at Ephesus

One of the things many people do each Sunday is "go to church." This has been something that has taken place for over 2000 years, once the shift was made to "go to church" or attend worship on Sundays as a result of the resurrection of Jesus Christ. The Apostle Paul makes the statement about giving in the "church" and says that we should do so *"upon the first day of the week"* which is actually Sunday.

I believe the body of Christ is due for a paradigm shift in its thinking concerning "church" as we understand it, because going to church is not what we do; being the church is who we are!

When Jesus was talking with His disciples one day, He asked them in Matthew 16:13, "... *Whom do men say that I the Son of man am?"* The disciples responded in verse 14, "*Some say that thou art John the Baptist; some Elias; and others Jeremias, or one of the prophets."* He then went on to ask them in verse 15, "*But whom say ye that I am?"* It was then that Simon Peter responded in verse 16, "*Thou art the Christ, the Son of the living God."* Once this revelation came to light, Jesus talked about the formation of the church when He said in verse 18, "*And I say also unto thee, That thou art Peter, and upon this rock I will build my church; and the gates of hell shall not prevail against it."* What was Jesus talking about here? It would appear to me that the Lord was not referring to a building where people assemble, but rather the people who would come to the knowledge of who He is that assemble in the building. He was talking about building His church on the "rock" or "foundation" of the knowledge that He (Jesus) is the Son of God and that those who confess Him as Lord and Savior would be known as the "church."

So the question I believe we need to ask at this point is "what is the church?" The word church comes from the Greek word *"ekklesia"* and is defined as "a calling out, i.e. (concretely) a popular meeting, especially a religious congregation (Jewish synagogue, or Christian community of members on earth or saints in heaven or both)."[1] I like the think of the church as the "called out ones" or those who have been removed from the *"wages of sin"* and have gone *"out of darkness and into His marvelous light."* It's not a building, but a living, a lifestyle, a way of life for those who have accepted Jesus the Christ as Lord and Savior. One day soon, Jesus is coming back for His church, the church that He purchased with His own blood, and we need

---

[1] Strong's Exhaustive Concordance of the Bible, Updated Edition

to ask ourselves the question, "will I be ready when He returns?" and if so, *__Which Church Are You?__*

The Book of Revelation is the last book of the Bible. Some people choose not to read it because of all the things that are prophesied to take place. For the Christian, if nothing else, when you know your Bible and the Book of Revelation, you can know at least two things: (1) there's a blessing in reading the book – as evidenced in Revelation 1:3; and (2) if you've accepted Jesus Christ as Lord and savior, you won't be here when the Great Tribulation takes place. God has truly blessed us with this book so we would know what will take place and to be ready for that season.

Our focus will be the seven churches in Asia Minor that Jesus is addressing in Chapters 2-3. Each church had its issues and problems, but they all had one thing in common...they were churches of Jesus Christ. If it is your intention to find a perfect church, you will never find it because the church is comprised of imperfect people. But what makes us special and unique is the fact that we have been forgiven, bought with a price, and washed in the blood of the lamb! Now that's something to shout about!

I want to call your attention to the church at Ephesus. The city of Ephesus was the most important city along the coast of Asia Minor. It was a great commercial city with a natural harbor and its strategic location made it as such because of the main road going through it. It wasn't a Christian city as the temple of the goddess Diana (the goddess of sensual pleasures) was there. We can say that even today there's nothing new under the sun because in the midst of all the churches located across the country, there are still temples of Diana all around – we just don't call them by that name anymore! Today they're call "Gentlemen's Clubs" or "Brothels" and somewhere close by you can find liquor stores located in the vicinity.

The churches were so important to Jesus that He took the time to address them and their actions. Let's see what He said to the Church at Ephesus. First, let's look at...

The Commendation (verses 2-3)

In these verses, Jesus commends or acknowledges the work of the Church at Ephesus and how they conducted themselves in certain areas. He commended them for their labor, for being patient, and for sticking with doctrine and not being "tossed to and fro" by false apostles. Let me help somebody here...just because somebody throws the title "apostle" or "pastor" or "Elder" or "Reverend" in front of their name does not mean they are faithfully working in that office for the Lord's kingdom. The Biblical requirements for the office of the Apostle can be found in the Book of Acts, Chapter 1. After the death of Judas, only Joseph called Barsabas and Matthias met the requirements of seeing Jesus before and after His resurrection, thus they met the requirement to be considered for the office of Apostle. Trust me, I understand the authority and sovereignty of the Lord, but I also understand that He is a God of order as well. I'm just saying...

Ephesus was a church that did not sit around and wait for somebody else to get it done; they got up and made things happen. I can imagine that they were the kind of people that didn't have the attitude like *"that's not my job so I'm not doing it."* Great things can happen in any organization when people work together to accomplish the stated mission. This was a working church, working for the kingdom of God to fulfill the commandments of God. I would venture to say that the church at Ephesus understood Scriptures like Matthew 25:35-36 which says, *"For I was hungered, and ye gave me meat: I was thirsty, and ye gave me drink: I was a stranger, and ye took me in; naked, and ye clothed me: I was sick, and ye visited me: I was in prison, and ye came unto me."* To keep this verse in context, Jesus was actually teaching His disciples that whenever they saw somebody in those predicaments - hungry, thirsty, a stranger, naked, etc., and did nothing about it, they were actually doing it to Him. It's a work that requires us to remember that God placed us here and has blessed us to be a blessing, and if we're going to be a blessing, we're going to have to do some work. I've learned that when we do the work for the Lord, we're letting our lights shine. Matthew 5:16 says, *"Let your light so shine before men, that they may see your good works, and glorify your Father which is in heaven."* When you're doing the Lord's work, you can anticipate **The Commendation**.

Next, He deals with…

The Complaint (verses 4-5)

Think about what was going on here – Jesus had just commended them for all the work they were doing, now He tells them He's got a problem with them! For some this would be the same as saying… *"you can't win for losing!"* I would submit that it's not completely about what you're doing, but rather how you're keeping things in perspective. The church was so busy doing the work of the Lord that they had really forgotten about the Lord of the work! Be mindful that the Lord is concerned about your work, but He's more concerned about your relationship with Him. Think about it... if you didn't have a relationship with Him, you wouldn't have a work to do for Him, would you? The Preachers Outline and Sermon Bible says here, *"The church and its believers had lost their feelings for Christ. The Greek says, "Your love the first [love]." Believers had left their first love. Christ was no longer first in their lives. They were putting themselves and their own affairs first, and they were putting the church first – the programs, services, ministries, and fellowship of the church. They had become more attached to the church than they were to Christ."*[2] I guess you can say they were *"going through the motions"* of what a church should look like, but they were not actively engaged with the founder of the church. We can never get to the point of thinking that "church" is all

---

[2] Preacher's Outline and Sermon Bible, Revelation, New Testament Volume 13

about us! And we should not go to "worship" to feel good, but rather we should go to "worship" to feel God!

Barbara Hughes asks the question, "*Why do we worship – for God or for ourselves? The unspoken but increasingly common assumption of today's average churchgoer is that worship is primarily for us – to meet our needs. Here's a telltale sign that this kind of thinking is prevalent. After service, everyone asks, 'What did you think of the service today? Or they slip out the door as quickly as possible. The real question should be 'what did God think of it – and of us? We ought to ask, 'What did I give to God?*"[3] So our worship cannot be world centered but God centered. We cannot become distracted by the things of the world and leave our first love. The Bible says in 1 John 2:15-17, "*Love not the world, neither the things that are in the world. If any man love the world, the love of the Father is not in him. For all that is in the world, the lust of the flesh, and the lust of the eyes, and the pride of life, is not*

---

[3]   Disciplines of a Godly Woman, Crossway Books, Wheaton, IL

of the Father, but is of the world. And the world passeth away, and the lust thereof: but he that doeth the will of God abideth for ever."

If you have left your first love and need to get things right with the Lord, all He wants you to do is confess and repent. Isaiah 55:7 says, *"Let the wicked forsake his way, and the unrighteous man his thoughts: and let him return unto the Lord, and he will have mercy upon him; and to our God, for he will abundantly pardon."*

When you have heard the complaint, and corrected it by repenting, then you can get ready for the last thing here which is...

The Promise (verse 7)

One thing (of all the things) I truly love about the Lord is that He will not leave you hanging! Once we meet His conditions, the blessings or whatever it is He has promised to us will be received. The promise here is that we will have the victory. The Preacher's Outline and Sermon Bible states, *"There is the promise to the overcomers. The word overcomer has the idea of conflict and struggle. The overcomer is the person who overcomes and conquers and gains victory. He is the victor and conqueror."*[4] A close examination of the text tells us that the overcomer has the privilege of partaking of the tree of life. This tree is in paradise and this is the place where God dwells.

❖ You can't get to God until you get to Jesus first;

❖ You can't get to Paradise until you get to Jesus first;

❖ You can't get to the tree of life until you get to Jesus first!

The Bible says in Revelation 22:2 that this tree will bare 12 manner of fruit, and yield one every month, and the leaves of the tree were for the healing of the nations.

One day, I'm going to make it to that tree, because my Jesus died on a tree that I would have ever lasting life. This is the same Jesus

---

[4]   Ibid

that is addressing the seven churches of the Book of Revelation.

- ❖ This is the same Jesus that said in Revelation 1:8, *"I am Alpha and Omega, the beginning and the ending, saith the Lord, which is, and which was, and which is to come, the Almighty."*
- ❖ This is the same Jesus that said in Revelation 1:18, *"I am he that liveth, and was dead; and, behold, I am alive for evermore, Amen; and have the keys of hell and of death."*
- ❖ This is the same Jesus that said in Revelation 22:12, *"And behold, I come quickly; and my reward is with me, to give every man according as his work shall be."*

He said all this after they hung Him high and stretched Him wide;
He said all this after He died on Calvary's cross;
He said all this after He was buried;
He said all this after He rose early on Sunday morning.

I don't want to just be busy; I want to be about my Father's business! I want to hear the Lord tell me one day... *"Well done, thou good and faithful servant: thou hast been faithful over a few things, I will make thee ruler over many things: enter thou into the joy of thy Lord!"* (Matthew 25:21)

If you want to hear the Lord utter those words, the question is ... **Which Church Are You? Are You Real or Just Going Through the Motions?**

Chapter 2

The Church at Smyrna

We're living in some crucial times. Trouble is everywhere; trials are everywhere; tribulations are everywhere. Here recently, we made it through the debt-ceiling fiasco during the Obama administration; politicians can't seem to work together for the good of the people they are supposed to be representing, and as time goes by, it seems like it's going to get worse before it gets better. The stock market plummeted in 2009 and investors weren't really sure where they needed to invest, and the east coast experienced an earthquake in 2011 and Hurricane Sandy in 2012. Most recently, our nation has been rocked with an onslaught of African-American men being killed at the hands of police officers, and now people are fighting back by killing police officers across the country. We're living in some crucial times!

Concerning the east coast earthquakes, the news showed pictures of some of the monuments in Washington, D.C. that we hold near and dear to our hearts as American citizens. These monuments showed evidence of falling apart because of the earthquake and when I saw them, what came to mind was how America is falling apart. I've said before that the further we've moved from Calvary, the further we're moving from God.

This is not a time to rely on man; this is truly a time to rely on God, and as the church of the Lord, we have to rely on what He has established for His church to do. I've said before that church is not where we go; church is who we are! The church is not an organization, comprised of by-laws, constitutions, and procedures – it's an organism that's alive, and exist for the glory of God. We who are part of the church should understand that God has placed us here to be light and salt, to show the world that knowing Jesus is not a bad thing; that knowing Jesus has its benefits; that knowing Jesus is the best relationship we can all be in.

Being in this relationship with Jesus will have its ups and downs, not because the Lord is unpredictable, but because life seems to come at you harder because you know Jesus!! The devil does not like the fact that you know Jesus, but that's his problem…not yours!!!

❖ There will be times when people will give you a hard time because of your faith;
❖ There will be times when people will question if you have faith; and,
❖ There will be times when you will need to exercise your faith.

When your faith is tested, remember who gave you your faith, that you are the church, and Jesus has your back! But to find out just what the Lord can do for you, you must find out...

Which Church Are You?

The word Smyrna means *bitter* and gets its name from myrrh, one of the chief commercial products of the city. Present day Smyrna is known as Izmir, a city on Turkey's Aegean coast.

The Church at Smyrna was a persecuted church. It was a church preaching and teaching Jesus Christ as Messiah, but the Jews in Smyrna – who were steeped in Old Testament Scriptures, did not accept Christ as the Messiah and gave that church a hard time. The Preacher's Outline and Sermon Bible says, *"Many of the early converts to Christ were Jews. Here in Smyrna, the reaction of the Jews was severe. They reacted severely and did all they could to influence the city officials to stamp out the church."*[5] That sounds a lot like what's

---

[5]   Ibid

happening today...we have groups of people who have their own agendas, and want their agenda to become everybody else's agenda. The Church of Smyrna was not following their own agenda, they were following directions from the founder of the Church that all men must come to repentance. They had their issues (as we all do) and the Lord had something to say to them. Let's see how He felt about Smyrna. First we have...

The Proclamation (verse 9)

Jesus proclaims to the Church at Smyrna that He knows what they are going through. He tells them He knows their works. Let me ask a question...are you working for the Lord? When the Day of Judgment comes, will you have something you can place at the foot of Jesus to show that you appreciate what He's done for you? Smyrna was also a working church, a church not afraid to tell people about their savior, and they went through tribulation for it. There are four things Jesus points out about this church.

❖ They met up with tribulation. The word "tribulation" comes from the Greek word "thlipsis"[6] which means pressure, afflicted, anguished, and burdened. Here the Lord acknowledges their tribulation and I'm reminded what Jesus said in Matthew 5:10 which says, *"Blessed are they which are persecuted for righteousness' sake; for theirs is the kingdom of God."* Even though they had tribulation, they remained faithful.

❖ They were poor. The Church at Smyrna had to deal with the loss of property, jobs, and a steady income. If you look at today's society, a lot of people could fall into the category of the Church of Smyrna because many people have lost their homes, jobs, and in a lot of cases, they've lost all hope too! Paul said in 2 Corinthians 8:9, *"For ye know the grace of our Lord Jesus Christ, that, though he was rich, yet for your sakes he became*

---

[6] Strong's Exhaustive Concordance of the Bible, Updated Edition

poor, that ye through his poverty might be rich."

❖ They were rich spiritually. Material things can make you happy, but it's a relationship with Jesus that can give you joy! We've got to be very careful about holding on to the things of this world because they are only temporary. The Bible says in Matthew 6:19-20, *"Lay not up for yourselves treasures upon earth, where moth and rust doth corrupt, and where thieves break through and steal; But lay up for yourselves treasures in heaven, where neither moth nor rust doth corrupt, and where thieves do not break through nor steal."*

❖ They were slandered. The rich Jews had a lot to say about the Church at Smyrna, even to the point of ridiculing them. The church today is taking a lot of ridicule, but we must hold on to the words of the Lord as found in Matthew 10:32-33 which says, *"Whosoever therefore shall confess me before me, him will I confess also before my Father which is in heaven. But whosoever therefore shall deny me before men, him will I deny before my Father which is in heaven."*

Next, we look at...

The Problem (verse 10)

The Lord here is letting the church know that they've already been through some things for His sake but more was to come. Most people don't like going through anything, but the reality is that you're *going* through is actually your *growing* through! It gives you an opportunity to see the mighty hand of God working in your life. Going through denotes a season and in this text, Jesus tells them it would last 10 days, thus referring to a beginning and an ending. One of the biggest problems with going through is fear – fear of failure; fear of the enemy; fear of the outcome; but Jesus encourages them to "fear not." Fear is not of God and when we operate in fear, we're actually operating outside of God. Jesus has already told them that He is the "first and the last" so He knows when it's going to start and when it will be over. As long as we know He's with us, we have no need to fear!! God told the children of Israel in Deuteronomy 31:6, *"Be strong and of a good courage, fear not, nor be afraid of them: for the Lord thy God, he it is that doth go with thee; he will not fail thee, nor forsake thee."*

❖ If you are operating in fear, it's time to tell fear where to get off at;

❖ If you are operating in fear, it's time to tell fear that you are more than a conqueror;

❖ If you are operating in fear, it's time to tell fear, "if God be for us, who can be against us?"

But you've got to go through to receive what's next and that is...

The Promise (verse 10)

Two things are promised to the overcomer – a crown of life, and deliverance from the second death.

The crown of life simply means eternal life. This is a life that has no ending whatsoever, and it's a blissful life with Jesus. 1 John 2:25 says, *"And this is the promise that he hath promised us, even eternal life."* And when you have the crown of life, you don't have to worry about the second death. The second death is reserved for all those who have rejected Jesus Christ as Lord and savior. Revelation 20:14 says, *"And death and hell were cast into the lake of fire. This is the second death."* The Preacher's Outline and Sermon Bible says here, *"The second death is the lake of fire, the judgment of eternal hell and torment from the presence of God forever and ever. The believer who overcomes in persecution shall escape the second death, the lake of fire and torment. The believer may have to pass through physical death, but he will never go through the second death. He shall be transported immediately into the presence of God to live forever and ever."*[7]

---

[7] Preacher's Outline and Sermon Bible, Revelation, New Testament, Volume 13

The Church at Smyrna was a working church; it was a faithful church; it was a church about the Father's business. Although it had some problems, it was still a church that Jesus was concerned about. If He was concerned about Smyrna, He's also concerned about you! You are the church of the Lord and He's got a promise for you too!! Be thou faithful unto death and you will receive a crown of life!!

Chapter 3

The Church at Pergamos

I am of the belief that the Lord does not need any help from the world to accomplish His mission and program here on earth. For example,

❖ Churches across the country are taking worldly songs, changing some of the words, and presenting them to the Lord during worship.

❖ Churches across the country are taking different styles of dancing, and presenting them to the Lord during worship.

There is no need to bring the things of the world into the church, but the church needs to make its presence known in the world! Some of the problems the church is faced with today is that it thinks it needs to identify itself with the world and actually it should be the other way around! The Bible teaches us that the Lord is coming back for His church; He already came to redeem the world, so the church doesn't need to bring the ways of the world into the church assembly. How many of us know that worldly ways can corrupt the church? Nothing will corrupt the church quicker than worldliness.

The church at Pergamos had some problems – much like the church today. It was faced with people who wanted to bring the world into the church and allow some to compromise the teachings of the Lord. I've said before that you must know for yourself what truth is and what's not the truth. Nowhere in Scripture does it says, "accept what people tell you what truth is" but rather we're commanded in 2 Timothy 2:15 to *"Study to show thyself approved unto God, a workman that needeth not to be ashamed, rightly dividing the word of truth."* When you don't know the truth, it becomes easy to compromise on something you don't hold near and dear to you. Although worldliness is out there, we who are the church must decide that we will not allow their ways to become our way of life, but do our best to allow the Lord to work through us and give them an opportunity to know the Lord for themselves. I've said before that the individual believer is the church and we must ask ourselves if we have allowed the world to corrupt us, or have we done our part to make an impact on the world. Jesus never allowed the world to consume Him, but by the time He was done in any location, people wanted to know Him better. The question that is still before us is, **Which Church Are You?**

Concerning the city of Pergamos, the Preacher's Outline and Sermon Bible says, *"Pergamos was a beautifully situated city with an air of royalty about it. It sat on top of a huge mountain, arising ever so steeply and majestically out of a beautiful valley. The city's citizens could see the Mediterranean Sea some fifteen miles away."*[8] How many of us know that everything that looks good, isn't good for us? This was a city in which Jesus was preached, but it was also a place where corruption ran rampant. Doesn't that sound a lot like today? People want to do the right thing but there's always somebody else around who has other things in mind. The church of today has that same issue – the mission is to preach and teach Jesus Christ as Lord and savior, but somebody or some group within the church always wants things done their way. It's been my personal observation over many years of attending churches that at times, pastoral direction, and even vision goes unaccomplished because somebody claims to have a better way. As I read through these letters, I find that the Lord is not talking to the congregation of believers, He's talking to

_____
[8]   Ibid

the *"angel of the church"* which is the minister or pastor.

First, the Lord starts off with...

The Compliment (verse 13)

The Lord makes it a point here to identify the things the church at Pergamos was doing right. Have you ever noticed that when you're doing right, wrong always seems to show up?

- ❖ You make it up in your mind to draw closer to the Lord and somebody interrupts you;
- ❖ You make it up in your mind to join a ministry and somebody has a problem with it;
- ❖ You make it up in your mind to study your Bible more and somebody questions you.

The Lord complimented this church for staying loyal to His name, for staying pure in doctrine, and for standing fast in persecution. The Lord makes reference to Satan's Seat, which, Dr. Albert Barnes says is *"a place of peculiar wickedness, as if Satan dwelt there. Satan is, as it were, enthroned there.*"[9] It would appear that the influence of Satan was strong in Pergamos and this church endured persecution. Even though they were attacked and persecuted, they still kept the faith. If you are going to be real in your relationship with Christ, be prepared for persecution. The Apostle Paul said in 2 Timothy 3:12, *"Yea, and all that will live godly in Christ Jesus shall suffer persecution."* But if you just hold on and stand fast in your faith, you can anticipate the blessings of the Lord. Paul also said in 2 Timothy 2:12, *"If we suffer, we shall also reign with him; if we deny him, he also will deny us."* I believe we all want to be complimented by the Lord, but be mindful that there will be a price to pay, knowing that a price has already been paid for us!

Next we have...

---

[9]   Barnes' Notes of the New Testament, Volume 15

The Criticism (verses 14-16)

Even though the Lord complimented this church, He found some things wrong with it. There were elements in the church who were guilty of following false doctrine and gross worldliness. To some degree, the church followed the doctrine of Christ, but also tolerated the doctrine of Balaam. This goes all the way back to the Book of Numbers when King Balac of Moab was afraid of Israel and sought the assistance of the prophet Balaam to curse Israel. Balaam went forth three times to curse Israel but to no effect, so Balac came up with a plan for the women to intermarry with the Israelite men and convinced them to seek after false gods. That same thing is happening today when you have people who say that Christianity is a lie and any other "religion" is the true religion. People are worshipping things, buildings, homes, cars, other people, or don't believe in anything but themselves. God said in Exodus 20:3, *"Thou shalt have no other gods before me."* Not only were they following that doctrine, but they were also participating in the doctrines of the Nicolaitanes. These people, according to Dr. Adam Clarke were *"a sect of the Gnostics, who taught the most impure doctrines and followed the most impure practices."*[10] Dr. Finis Dake adds that the Nicolaitanes *"practices and taught impure and immoral doctrines, such as the community of wives, that committing adultery and fornication was not sinful, and that eating meats offered to idols was lawful."*[11] Jesus had a problem with them because they tolerated such practices. The Lord told the church at Pergamos to repent, or in other words, turn away from their evil ways. He also commanded us through the Apostle Paul in 2 Corinthians 6:14, *"Be ye not unequally yoked together with unbelievers: for what fellowship hath righteousness with unrighteousness? And what communion hath light with darkness?"* I don't know about you, but I don't want the Lord to complain about me; I don't want the Lord to be disappointed with me; I don't want the Lord

---

[10] Adam Clarke's Commentary of the Bible
[11] Dake's Annotated Reference Bible

to find fault in me. One of the things we can take solace in is found in Psalm 1:1-2 where we find, *"Blessed is the man that walketh not in the counsel of the ungodly, nor standeth in the way of sinners, nor sittest in the seat of the scornful. But his delight is in the law of the Lord; and in his law doth he meditate day and night."*

When you've heard the compliment, and have been made aware of the complaint and criticism, you can anticipate what's next and that's...

The Promise (verse 17)

There's a promise from the Lord for all overcomers. If you are in Jesus, you are already an overcomer and the Lord has made promises to the overcomers. He promised them hidden manna. Dr. Warren Wiersbe says here, *"Instead of eating 'things sacrificed to idols' (Revelation 2:14), the believers in Pergamos needed to feast on God's holy food, the bread of life found in Jesus Christ through the Word."*[12] Jesus himself said in John 6:51, *"I am the living bread which*

---

[12]   The Bible Exposition Commentary, New Testament, Volume 2

came down from heaven: if any man eat of this bread, he shall live for ever: and the bread that I will give is my flesh, which I will give for the life of the world."

Not only does the overcomer get manna, but a white stone with a new name on it. Concerning the white stone, Dr. Finis Dake writes, *"These were known to the ancients as victory stones. Also in ancient times they meant pardon and the evidence of it. Judges had white and black stones. If a black one was given the criminal he was condemned; if a white stone, he would be pardoned."*[13]

One day, the Lord will give each overcomer a white stone with a new name on it. I don't know what the name will be, but I can imagine that new name might be "redeemed"; that new name might be "forgiven"; that name might be "my child." Regardless as to what the name is, it lets us know that the Lord is keeping His promise.

---

[13]   Dake's Annotated Reference Bible

I'm talking about Jesus:

> The author and finisher of our faith;
>
> The joy of my salvation;
>
> The Lamb of God;
>
> The Redeemer of our souls;
>
> The King of kings; and
>
> The Lord of lords;
>
> The Captain of our salvation; and,
>
> The Prince of Peace.

I'm talking about the One that said in Revelation 1:18, *"I am he that liveth, and was dead; and behold, I am alive for evermore, Amen; and have the keys of hell and of death."*

He's Jesus the Christ, the Son of the Living God!!

Chapter 4

The Church at Thyatira

In this day and times we're living in, we must be very careful of "outside influences." These are the things that will try to convince you that there's another way or a better way of doing things, and normally those are the things that don't line up with truth or better yet, the will and Word of God. "Outside Influences" have the potential to cause you to compromise your principles or standards. To understand this, we must take a trip all the way back to the first book of the Bible when God placed Adam and Eve in the Garden of Eden and told them what they could eat and what they couldn't eat. Everything was going well until an "outside influence" showed up to sway them to do what God had told them not to do. God told Adam they could eat of every fruit of the garden except the fruit of the tree of good and evil. The consequences of his disobedience would result in death. The "outside influence" that showed up in the Garden of Eden was the devil himself, in the form of a serpent, and he mixed a lie with the truth and made it look real good. It is so important for us to understand that the devil only wants to *"steal, kill and destroy,"* but we have power over him in Jesus Christ! The devil began to provide them with options or alternatives and told them they would not die. Eve was deceived, Adam ate, and we've been in trouble ever since! You see:

❖ Marriages are torn apart because of "outside influences;"

❖ Families are torn apart because of "outside influences;"

❖ Churches are torn apart because of "outside influences!"

The way you combat "outside influences" is that you know the truth for yourself and apply that truth to your life on a daily basis.

The church at Thyatira had an "outside influence" and Jesus made them aware of it. This outside influence caused them to compromise their principles and they suffered as a result of it. It might be easy to get distracted, but it's better to keep your eyes on Jesus and the blessings He has promised you. The question remains...***Which Church Are You?***

The city of Thyatira was known as a frontier town – a town that had no defensible surroundings and if something were to break out, they had to wait on the citizens of Pergamos to help them out. Concerning the church at Thyatira, it is believed that this was the smallest of the seven churches mentioned, yet it received the longest letter from the Lord. Because this was a compromising church, Christ had more to say to it than the other six churches. Compromise can lead to catastrophe!! It is said that *"a little leaven leaventh the whole lump!"*[14]

Let's see what the Lord had to say to the church at Thyatira. He starts off by talking about...

The Redeemer (verse 18)

In each of the letters to the various churches, Jesus gives a description of Himself to the church. To this church, He refers to Himself as *"The Son of God, who hath his eyes like unto a flame of fire, and his feet are like fine brass."* Notice if you will what He says about Himself:

1. <u>He refers to Himself as the Son of God</u>. He is the One we all owe our lives to. He's the giver of life; He's the sustainer of life; He's the provider of life; He is life itself!!! Because He is the Son of God, that teaches us we can't compromise because He didn't compromise! The Bible

---

[14] 1 Corinthians 5:6

teaches us in Matthew 4 that the Holy Spirit sent Jesus forth to be tempted of the devil. He (the devil) tried the same thing on Jesus that he tried on Adam, but this time it wasn't going to work. In verses 3 and 6, the devil said, *"If thou be the Son of God..."* Jesus came back to him with, *"It is written..."* In verse 9, the devil said, *"All these things will I give thee, if thou wilt fall down and worship me."* Jesus tells the devil in verse 10, *"Get thee hence, Satan, for it is written, Thou shalt worship the Lord thy God, and him only shalt thou serve."* You see, that word "if" is a powerful word because it can lead to compromise. As the Son of God, He's the One we must worship, not the things of the world, not the people of the world, not the possession and riches of the world. Jesus said in Luke 9:23, *"If any man will come after me, let him deny himself, and take up his cross daily, and follow me."*

2. <u>He says that His eyes are like a flame of fire.</u> This gives us an indication that Christ

sees all. Proverbs 15:3 reminds us that *"The eyes of the Lord are in every place, beholding the evil and the good."* You see, most times, we think we're getting away with stuff because nobody (physically) sees what we do, but the reality is that God sees us all the time. The Preacher's Outline and Sermon Bible says here, *"Christ sees all. He sees when a person is compromising, compromising in the dark, behind closed doors, in parked cars, in the offices and houses of the world. He sees all compromise that lies, steals, cheats, commits immorality, becomes intoxicated, takes drugs. He sees all the seductive teaching and misleading of people within the church."*[15] This was actually a way for the Lord the let the church at Thyatira know that He was aware of their compromising. Jesus himself said in Luke 12:2-3, *"For there is nothing covered, that shall not be revealed; neither hid that shall*

---

[15] Preacher's Outline and Sermon Bible, Revelation, New Testament Volume 13

not be known. Therefore, whatsoever ye have spoken in darkness shall be heard in the light; and that which ye have spoken in the ear of closets shall be proclaimed upon the housetops." Fire has the power to tear through some stuff and destroy whatever it touches and in the case of Thyatira, the Lord was preparing them for what would take place.

3. <u>Christ said His Feet are like Brass</u>. Again, the Preacher's Outline and Sermon Bible says here, *"Christ is able to step down hard upon all seductive teaching and compromise. He rules and He judges. His feet shall crush all those who compromise with the world. In addition, His feet shall crush all false teachers of compromise. The reason is clear: He is the only true spokesman and messenger of God. All others are false. Therefore, they must be judged and cursed."*[16] Christ is saying that He alone has the power to step on and stomp out all unrighteousness and bring

---

[16]   Ibid

about judgment. The Bible says in Psalm 96:13, *"Before the Lord: for he cometh, for he cometh to judge the earth: he shall judge the world with righteousness, and the people with his truth."*

Next He deals with...

The Reason (verses 20-25)

In verse 19, Jesus tells the church at Thyatira that He's aware of their works, their charity, their service, their faith, and their patience; but in the midst of all they were doing, He still had a reason to write to them because of their discrepancies. We've all heard the statement, "nobody's perfect" and we use that as a crutch to do what WE want to do instead of what God wants done. Yes, Romans 3:23 says, *"For all have sinned and come short of the glory of God,"* but that does not give us blanket authority to do whatever we think we're big and bad enough to do. Jesus had a problem with the Church of Thyatira because they allowed an "outside influence" to come in and convince them to do things another way. Jesus mentions a woman named *"Jezebel which calleth herself a prophetess"* and how they allowed her to teach them false doctrines. The best way to counter false doctrine is by knowing the truth! He said that Jezebel began *"to teach and to seduce my servants to commit fornication, and to eat things sacrificed unto idols."* You see,

❖ She taught them false doctrines;
❖ She taught them to commit adultery;
❖ She taught them to eat foods offered up to idols.

These were things that the people of God and the church was taught not to do; yet they allowed her to convince them otherwise. The problem with this is that the church was allowing or tolerating this type of teaching to take place, and compromise has been tolerated ever since. When you don't know the truth, you will follow anything somebody tells you. By her deceptive ways and devices, she was able to convince members in the church to do what she said, and not what the Lord commanded. The Apostle

Paul reminds us in Romans 12:2, *"Be not conformed to this world, but be ye transformed by the renewing of your minds, that ye may prove what is that good, and acceptable, and perfect will of God."* We have the responsibility of learning and knowing the truth, which will enable us to become walking epistles of the Lord Jesus Christ.

Notice what the Lord says about Jezebel in verse 21, *"And I gave her space to repent of her fornication; and she repented not."* Even though she did all these wrong things, notice the mercy of the Lord towards her. He gave her a chance to repent, but she chose not to. Jesus imposed judgment on her, her followers, and her children and again, the Apostle Paul gives us understanding as to how the Lord deals with these types of people. Romans 2:5-6 says, *"But after thy hardness and impenitent heart treasurest up unto thyself wrath against the day of wrath and revelation of the righteous judgment of God; Who will render to every man according to his deeds."* The Amplified Bible puts it this way, *"But by your callous stubbornness and impenitence of heart you are storing up wrath and indignation for yourself on the day of wrath and indignation, when God's righteous judgment (just doom) will be revealed. For He will render to every man according to his works [justly, as his deeds deserve]."*[17] In other words, she reaped what she sowed and that principle still applies to us today. God hasn't changed; His Word hasn't changed; His principles haven't changed; and for those who will not repent and receive Christ as Lord and savior, the judgment reserved for the wicked hasn't changed either!!

Lastly, the Lord deals with...

The Reward (verse 26-28)

There is a promise to the overcomer, the one who recognizes the outside influence which causes compromise, and does not bow down to it. Two things are promised here to the overcomer:

1. The Overcomer is given power over nations. The understanding here is that the

---

[17] The Amplified Bible

overcomer will be given the opportunity to rule and reign with Jesus throughout all eternity. Things of this world can make you feel good for a little while; but what Jesus has for us will give us joy for all eternity. The mindset of an overcomer is one who endures for the cause of Christ. 2 Timothy 2:12 says, *"If we suffer, we shall also reign with him; if we deny him, he also will deny us."*

2. <u>The Morning Star.</u> The second promise the overcomer will receive is the Morning Star, or Jesus Himself. The Bible teaches us in Revelation 22:16 that Jesus is the *"bright and morning star."* That means that if we will just hold on, we will receive the reward of the Lord from the Lord.

The Church at Thyatira compromised, but Jesus gave them a choice. That choice is still available to anyone today who has compromised in their beliefs, or compromised in their principles, or compromised in doctrine.

❖ The choice is to come to Jesus, the founder of the church and the author and finisher of our faith;

❖ The choice is to come to Jesus, the faithful and just one;

❖ The choice is to come to Jesus, the creator and sustainer of life;

❖ The choice is to come to Jesus, the One who gave His life that we might have everlasting life;

❖ The choice is to come to Jesus, the One who rose early Sunday morning with all power in His hands.

❖ The choice is to come to Jesus, the One who one day will return again, at which time, every knee shall bow, and every tongue shall confess that Jesus Christ is King of kings and Lord of lords.

If you want to see Jesus one day, you've got to answer the question…***Which Church Are You***!!

Chapter 5

The Church at Sardis

Thus far, we've looked at the first four churches that Jesus addressed in Asia Minor. Each church had its issues, its problems, its areas that needed work. In looking at those churches, we find that:

- ❖ Ephesus was a *loving* church;
- ❖ Smyrna was a *persecuted* church;
- ❖ Pergamos was a *worldly* church; and,
- ❖ Thyatira was a *compromising* church.

I've said before that although they had their problems, they were still churches of Jesus Christ and He loved them enough to tell them about themselves. Most people don't want to hear the negative things that people observe in them, but a person who truly loves you will tell you in such a way that they're trying to help you and not hurt you. Concerning God's love for us, we're told in Hebrews 12:6, *"For whom the Lord loveth he chasteneth, and scourgeth every son whom he receiveth."* With these seven churches, Jesus is taking the time to tell them about themselves so that repentance and change can take place. Again, the first step to solving a problem is to identify the problem, then take the steps necessary to correct it. We must be very careful in our work for the Lord and never get to the point that this work is all about me, the way I want to do it, the way I think it should be done, the way I'm going to make it happen. The reality is that it's not even our work...this work belongs to the Lord and we should consider it a privilege to be provided the opportunity to do the Lord's work. We must remember that the Lord is not getting His work done through the world – He's getting it done through His church. So let's ask ourselves the question... *"**Which Church Are You?**"*

Jesus is continuing to deal with the seven of the churches in Asia Minor. Each time the Lord addressed any of the seven churches, He pointed out that He knew their works, and then begins to identify their problems. In the case of the church of Sardis, He stated that they were a dead church. What exactly is a dead church? My personal observation of a dead church is a church that is satisfied with itself, what it has accomplished, and does not desire to grow in the Lord. It has lost its drive and desire to see others come to the saving power of Jesus, and is content with the fact that, "I've got mine!" When you look at the Scriptures, you will find that the Lord never told us to *"come and sit"* but actually we're told to *"go and get!"* A dead or dying church is a busy church, but it's busy doing programs, busy doing activities, busy doing something, but it's not busy enough sharing Jesus with the unsaved. A dead or dying church is a cold church – when visitors come by, they receive a cold reception, sit on a cold pew, and get the cold shoulder from people. Obviously, this is not what the Lord intended for His church. Isaiah 29:13 says, *"Wherefore the Lord said, Forasmuch as this people draw near me with their mouth, and with their lips do honor me, but have removed their heart far from me, and their fear toward me is taught by the precept of men."*

So let's see what the Lord says to the Church at Sardis. He starts off with…

The Complaint (verse 1)

Notice what Jesus says here to the church at Sardis…He said He knows their works and that they have a name that they are alive, but actually they are dead! They give the appearance of being a church; they come across looking like a church; they meet when churches normally meet; they say the things the church is supposed to say; yet they don't have anything spiritually to show for it. Lives are not being changed; souls are not being saved; families are not being helped; they're living off the accomplishments of the past and forgetting that there's more work to be done in the future. The Preacher's Outline and Sermon Bible says here, "...*it means...*

- *To have a form of worship but to deny the power thereof (2 Timothy 3:5);*
- *To focus upon ritual, ceremony, and worship instead of Jesus Christ;*
- *To focus upon activities instead of Jesus Christ;*
- *To become formal in worship instead of alive in Christ;*
- *To conduct activities in order to keep the organization going instead of learning about Christ and sharing about Christ;*
- *To lose one's zeal for witnessing and sharing Christ and seeing others grow;*
- *To become complacent and lethargic in the study of God's Word and in prayer and spiritual growth;*

- *To sit in worship and Bible classes as a matter of form instead of hungering and thirsting after righteousness;*
- *To preach and teach as a matter of form;*
- *To use the ministry as a means of livelihood instead of preaching and teaching to win and grow people in Christ.*"[18]

The bottom line is that the Lord does not want us to meet for the sake of meeting, but meet with worship on our minds and hearts and thanksgiving on our lips. Titus 1:16 is a great Scripture that deals with a dead church. The Scripture reads, *"They profess that they know God; but in works they deny him, being abominable, and disobedient, and unto every good work reprobate."* Jesus had a problem with it then, and I believe He has a problem with it today. I believe we all must do some soul searching, some self-examination, and ask ourselves the question... "Can the Lord complain about my works and my worship?"

Next He deals with...

---

[18]   Ibid

The Correction (verses 2-3)

We must all remember the grace and mercy of God. When we won't do right and find ourselves on the other side of God's judgment, grace and mercy steps in to give us another chance. Here the Lord tells them to do two things... be watchful, and strengthen the things that remain. What the Lord was telling them was that although there were some dead things out there, they could still be revived and they needed to strengthen those things to bring them back to life. You see, it's one thing to do the Lord's work by going through the motions, but it's another thing all together to "go through the motions and call it the Lord's work." I read somewhere where they said the folks at Sardis were, "...*sitting in the services half asleep and allowing their thoughts to wander about instead of hungering for the Word of God.*"[19] They were "...*holding and attending the activities for the sake of fellowship and because it was the thing to do.*"[20] The Prophet Jeremiah said in 48:10,

---

[19] Anonymous
[20] Anonymous

"*Cursed be he that doeth the work of the Lord deceitfully.*" In James 4:17 we find, "*Therefore to him that knoweth to do good, and doeth it not, to him it is sin.*" Jesus told the church at Sardis that if they didn't get their act together, He would come back without their knowledge and "handle His business!" When the Lord brings correction, it's so we can receive the rewards He's promised us, so therefore, it brings us back into a right standing with the Lord.

We've talked about the Complaint, and we've looked at the Correction; now let's look at the third thing here which is...

The Promise (verses 4-5)

The Lord promises here that the overcomers would wear white raiment, which would indicate to us that some people in the church of Sardis did not defile themselves like the others; some of the people were real with their worship; some of the people were sincere in their love and work for the Lord. White always denotes purity and being unblemished.

❖ Only those that did things Christ's way would wear the white raiment;

❖ Only those that were faithful to Christ and not to man, and not to programs, and not to traditions that were unbiblical and not trying to be men pleasers would wear white raiment.

Then He makes a reference to the Book of Life. The Apostle John says in Revelation 20:12, *"And I saw the dead, small and great, stand before God; and the books were opened: and another book was opened, which is the book of life: and the dead were judged out of those things which were written in the books, according to their works."* A close examination of this text tells us that the dead are judged from the books, but the righteous are judged from the Book of Life. There were some dead folks in Sardis, and there were some folks who were on fire for the Lord. Which book do you want to be judged from? I like what Jesus says here – He said if you overcome, He won't blot your name out of the book of life, but will also confess your name before God the Father. He's vouching for your faithfulness; He's vouching for your stewardship; He's vouching for your sincerity; He's vouching for your endurance; He's vouching for your ability to overcome with Him as your source and strength.

One day, we're going to stand before the Lord; one day, we're going to have to give an account before the Lord; one day, He's going to let us know some things about ourselves; one day, He's going to tell us where we stand. He's got a right to judge us because He's earned that right.

To redeem us, someone had to die, and Jesus was the only One qualified to fit the bill;

Not only did He die, but He was buried for your sins and mine;

Not only buried, but He's the only One who got up early on Sunday morning with all power in His hands.

He's the Way; He's the Truth; and He's the Life.

He's Jesus...nobody greater; nobody greater than Jesus!!!

Chapter 6

The Church at Philadelphia

———————◇◆◇———————

From a natural perspective, I believe all of us have gone to a concert or two in our lifetime. When you heard the group was coming to town, you made it a point to get your tickets early so you could get a great seat. This same principle applies to plays, movies, and anything that has the potential to entertain us. We were excited when we got there and expected to be excited when we left. If the band, group, play, movie, or whatever it was didn't excite us, we said it was "dead" and were disgusted that we spent good money on a "dead" event. From a worldly perspective, we wanted to be entertained. From a Christian perspective, attending worship is never intended to entertain, but rather draw us closer in our relationship with God. We do that through our time of praise and worship, the singing of songs that acknowledge and glorify our God, and encourage us to keep our hands on the "gospel plow." Worship should therefore be a "lively" event because of the status of the founder of the church.

The Bible teaches us that our Lord and Savior Jesus Christ was crucified on a cross. We're also told that He was buried in a borrowed tomb, and that on the third day He rose from the dead with all power in His hands. Jesus made a statement in John 2:19 which said, "...*Destroy this temple and in three days, I will raise it up.*" When He made that statement, He was not referring to the physical temple that had taken the people forty-six years to build, but He was referring to His body. We have Biblical accounts of our Lord being seen of various people after His resurrection which attests to His resurrection power. I share this because we serve a risen savior who is alive forever more. He is the founder of the church and wants His church to be alive or lively. Somebody once said, *"Anything that is dead should be buried."* Jesus is coming back again for His church and He's looking for a church that is alive and about the Father's business. When the question is asked, *"Which Church Are You?"*, can you honestly say that you are a church that is alive or a church that has resigned itself to just being saved and that's enough for you? There are some denominations that teach that people must work in order to earn their salvation. That is not the case for the Christian faith because according to Ephesians 2:8-9, *"For by grace are ye saved through faith; and that not of yourselves: it is the gift of God: Not of works, lest any man should boast."* We don't work to be saved...we're saved to go to work for the Kingdom. And anything dead, can't work!!

Turning our attention to the Church at Philadelphia, the word "Philadelphia" means "brotherly love" so it would stand to reason that this church would be one to show love to one another. I'm not talking about a "Sunday only" love that takes place all too often, but a love that is shown and felt on every day that ends in the letter "y." Love is an action word so in order to love you have to be alive and in motion. The Church at Philadelphia was not a dead church like Sardis, but was alive and wanted to honor its Lord and Savior. The Lord made it a point to address this church in such a way that they understood who was speaking to them. He identified Himself as the holy one, the true one, the one who had the keys of David, and having keys signifies power and authority. You do know God the Father stated that Jesus would sit on the seat of David and that His kingdom would be an everlasting kingdom?

I don't know about you, but that sounds like power and authority to me!!

Writing to the Church at Philadelphia, there are three areas the Lord addresses to them. First we have..

The Commendation (verse 8)

In commending them, He said...

- ❖ He knew their works;
- ❖ He said they had little strength;
- ❖ He said they kept His word;
- ❖ He said they have not denied His name.

This was a church that was alive and doing those things necessary for the kingdom. When you're doing the right things, you should anticipate hearing a good report for your efforts. The Apostle Paul reminds us in 1 Corinthians 15:58, *"Therefore, my beloved brethren, be ye steadfast, unmoveable, always abounding in the work of the lord, forasmuch as ye know that your labour is not in vain in the Lord."* Dr. J. Vernon McGee says here, *"The Lord Jesus is looking for fruit; He is looking for works in the lives of believers.*"[21] He further says, "*...there is something wrong with your faith if it doesn't produce works. Saving faith produces works.*"[22] John Calvin, one of the church fathers of the 16th century said, "*Faith alone saves, but faith that saves is not alone.*" The exercise of our faith requires us to be in motion, thus we must be a church that is alive in order to make something happen for the kingdom.

Even though they had a little strength, that didn't stop them from keeping His word and not denying His name. If we're not careful, we'll find an excuse not to do something...the conditions aren't right; you don't have everything you think you need; things are not the way they used to be; somebody might be in your way; regardless of the obstacles, it doesn't excuse us from doing what's right in the sight of the Lord. Jesus commended this church because of its ability to "keep on keeping on" and that's something we can all do today. I believe it's

---

[21] Thru The Bible, Volume V
[22] Ibid

time for us to stop letting our obstacles tell us how big they are, and time for us to start telling our obstacles how big our God is! His word declares in Ephesians 3:20 that He is *"able to do exceeding abundantly above all that we ask or think, according to the power that worketh in us."* They weren't concerned about what was going on...they relied on the fact that they were a church of Jesus Christ and His presence and power was with them. Faith opens up the door of the manifested power of the Lord which is why Paul said in 2 Corinthians 5:7, *"For we walk by faith, not by sight."* A walking by faith church is an alive church and that's what the Lord is looking for when He returns.

Next He deals with...

The Counsel (verse 9)

Although the Church at Philadelphia was commended for being alive, the Lord still found some things that needed adjustments in the church. Here the Lord makes a reference to the synagogue of Satan and the ones who call themselves Jews, but were not. He said they lie! Listen, if you recall, Jesus is talking to the pastor of the church and is saying that there are some folks within the church who in today's vernacular, are church folks and not Christians. This is a clear indicator that not everyone who comes into the house of the Lord is there to worship the Lord in spirit and in truth. Here are some attributes of church folks:

- ❖ They call themselves Christians;
- ❖ They act like Christians are supposed to act;
- ❖ They attend worship at the designated times;
- ❖ They say what Christians are supposed to say;

Yet the Lord says they are not who they say they are! The Lord saw it then, and He still sees it now! He knows who the real Christians are; He knows who the faithful Christians are; He knows the Christians who are "all in" and not just *part-time members in a full time church!* We find in 1 Samuel 16:7, "*...for the*

Lord seeth not as man seeth; for man looketh on the outward appearance, but the Lord looketh on the heart."

He went on to say that those very same people would one day bow down before His feet and know that He loved His church. We don't know when that will take place, but we should be mindful that it's time out for playing church. The Apostle Paul said in Romans 14:11, *"For it is written, As I live, saith the Lord, every knee shall bow to me, and every tongue shall confess to God."* Folks may be playing today, but one day, playing will be over; folks may be faking today, but one day, faking will be over; folks may be perpetrating today, but one day, perpetrating will be over. Every knee shall bow, and every tongue shall confess!!

Then He finishes with...

The Promise (verse 12)

The Lord always makes sure we know what to expect when we get ourselves in obedience. Here He says He will make the overcomers to become pillars in the temple of God. A pillar is a column that stands and supports the structure of the building. It takes a lot to knock down or knock over a pillar because of its foundation. Can you imagine the Lord telling us that as we overcome, He will make us into pillars that stand for the kingdom; pillars that stand on His authority; pillars that stand on His power and ability? The Preacher's Outline and Sermon Bible says here, *"They will be made a pillar in the temple of God. This means they will become a permanent part of God's house, of the eternal worship and service of heaven."*[23] The promise is that we will be in His presence throughout all eternity and that's something worth obtaining from the Lord.

He then went on to say that He would write upon the overcomer the name of His God. I don't know what name He's going to write, but I can imagine some of the names that have already been revealed to us. Names like:

---

[23] Preacher's Outline and Sermon Bible, Revelation, New Testament, Volume 13

❖ Jehovah-Elohim, the Eternal Creator;

❖ Adonai-Jehovah, The Lord our Sovereign;

❖ Jehovah-Jireh, the Lord our Provider;

❖ Jehovah-Nissi, the Lord our Banner;

❖ Jehovah-Ropheka, the Lord our Healer;

❖ Jehovah-Shalom, the Lord our Peace;

❖ Jehovah-Tsidkeenu – the Lord our Righteousness;

❖ Jehovah-Saboath, the Lord of Hosts;

❖ Jehovah-Shammah, the Lord is Present;

❖ Jehovah-Elyon, the Lord Most High;

❖ Jehovah-Rohi, the Lord my Shepherd;

❖ Jehovah-Hoseenu, the Lord our Maker;

❖ Jehovah-Eloheenu, the Lord our God;

❖ Jehovah-Eloheka, the Lord thy God; and,

❖ Jehovah-Elohay, the Lord my God!!

Whichever name He uses, it's good enough for me!

I like the name "Lamb of God" because He became a ransom for many;
I like the name "Redeemer," because He redeemed us from our sins;

I like the name "King of kings" because there's nobody else like Him;
I like the name "Lord of lords" because He's got all power in His hands.

When He comes back to get His church, the question that must be answered is...***Which Church Are You?***

Chapter 7

The Church at Laodicea

I believe no one likes being around people who are "wishy-washy." I'm talking about people who are one way today, and another way tomorrow. These are the type of people you really don't know what to expect from them because one day they might be hot, and the next day, they might be cold. You know how it is,

❖ They say one thing one day, and will say something entirely different the next day.

❖ They say they got your back, but are standing at the ready to stab you in the back.

❖ They give you the impression that they are one way, but when you see them at some other time, they are another way all together.

James 1:8 says, *"A double-minded man is unstable in all his ways."* Because they are neither one nor the other, they can be considered "lukewarm."

If you give it any real thought, a person who is considered "lukewarm" is one who has one foot in the house of the Lord and one foot in the world. When something comes by that catches their attention, regardless as to what side it takes place on, that's the side they will go on. They don't take into account that spending too much time on the world's side will in fact have consequences they will have to deal with. We must understand that the devil would love nothing more than to be able to say that the people of God are lukewarm, that they want to live the way they want to live, yet when you talk to them, they want God to bless them every day of their lives, regardless how they live!

It's been my observation that a lukewarm church looks a lot like a church, but looks a whole lot like the world too. It's no wonder the unchurched can't seem to tell the difference from what the real church of Jesus Christ looks like and a church that looks a whole lot like the world. You've probably heard some of the things they say about a lukewarm church. They say things like:

- **_"I don't go to church because they are a bunch of hypocrites_.**" They say that because they see people from the church hanging out in the bar, hanging out in the club, or if you listen to them long enough, you can't tell which one is saved or which one still needs to be saved! The unchurched are looking for a reason to stay away, and we should do our best not to give it to them.

- **_"I don't go to church because all the preacher wants is my money."_** A statement like that tells us they don't understand who owns everything and will blame somebody so they will have an excuse not to attend worship. Our responsibility is to share with them the truths of God's word and live it in front of them.

- **_"I don't go to church because it lasts too long."_** It's interesting to me that they will say worship lasts a long time, but if they attended their favorite sporting event, or had a chance to spend the day at the mall or whatever, they wouldn't complain about that. God gives us 168 hours a week and for me, there's nothing wrong with enjoying the presence of the Lord for a few hours on a Sunday morning. I don't only want to feel His presence just on Sunday, I want to feel His presence every day of my life. I can't speak for anybody else, but when I leave worship, I feel better, I have a better outlook on life, and I appreciate the fact that God inhabits the praises of His people.

- **"*I don't go to church because there's nothing wrong with my life*.**" Obviously, this is someone that doesn't understand what they are saying, nor do they understand what's really going on in their lives. We're all "sinners saved by grace" and need the saving power of the Lord to touch our lives on a daily basis. Because they don't really understand what has happened in their past, they can't see what the future holds for them. It's our job as the body of Christ to let them know that Jesus died for the opportunity to help them with their futures.

The Lord is not calling us to "luke warmness;" He's calling us to *faithfulness* in Him and the kingdom of God.

In these last and evil days we're living in, we who are the church must ask ourselves the question...**Which Church Are You?**

We're looking at the very last church the Lord addressed, which is the Church at Laodicea. In addressing this church, we find that the Lord didn't have anything nice to say about it at all. He told them that He knew their works, but that's as far as it went. Can you imagine a church that you can't find anything good to say about it? I'm talking about a church that is:

* ❖ Indifferent; meaning without interest or concern; not caring;
* ❖ Complacent; meaning pleased with itself or its accomplishments;
* ❖ Lethargic; meaning sluggish or drowsy;
* ❖ Half-hearted; meaning having or showing little enthusiasm; and,
* ❖ Half-committed; meaning only putting forth minimum effort instead of doing all as unto the Lord.

It's because of the problems He found in the church that He starts of with…

The Complaint (verses 15-16)

Because the Lord didn't have anything good to say about the church at Laodicea, He cut to the chase and began to tell them about themselves. He told them that they were a "lukewarm church." The Preacher's Outline and Sermon Bible says a few things about a lukewarm church. They say...

❖ "A lukewarm church is only half-committed to Jesus Christ. In addition to stressing Christ, it stresses ritual, ceremony, and programs as a way to become acceptable and to please God.

❖ A lukewarm church is only half-committed to proclaiming that Jesus Christ is the Son of God.

❖ A lukewarm church is only half-committed to teaching the Word of God.

❖ A lukewarm church is only half-committed to evangelism and missions.

❖ A lukewarm church is only half-committed to stressing holy and pure living for Christ.

❖ A lukewarm church is only half-committed to self-denial and sacrificial living, to stressing that its people must deny themselves and sacrificially die to self. They seldom stress that total sacrifice is demanded that a person must give all he is and has to reach the lost and meet the desperate needs of the world.

❖ A lukewarm church is only half-committed to the church.

❖ A lukewarm church is only half-committed to attending and staying awake and learning in the services of the church.

❖ A lukewarm church is only half-committed to supporting the church.

❖ A lukewarm church is only half-committed to witnessing.

❖ A lukewarm church is only half-committed to Bible study and prayer.

❖ A lukewarm church is only half-committed to daily devotions."[24]

---

[24] Preacher's Outline and Sermon Bible, Revelation, Volume 13, Outline Only

The Lord is looking for someone who will be obedient to what He said in Luke 9:23 which says, *"...If any man will come after me, let him deny himself, and take up his cross daily, and follow me."* It means letting go of the things of this world, and holding fast to the things of Christ. We're reminded in 1 John 2:15, *"Love not the world, neither the things that are in the world."* Jesus told this church that He would spew or spit this church out of His mouth because of their actions and disobedience. But He has a word for them...

The Counsel (verses 17-19)

Here Jesus continues to tell them about themselves. When you have a church that is satisfied with itself, it will always talk about what they've done or what they have, but will not talk about what they could be doing. Jesus tells them that even though they think they have a lot, the reality is that they have nothing without Him. It's easy to say that *"we've got a nice building"* or to say *"we've got X amount of members"*, or to say, *"We give big money to the* poor," but if you don't have Jesus, you really don't have anything. Think about what He said... *"buy of me gold tried in the fire."* He's not talking about physical gold, but rather He's referring to them sincerely trying Him and His redemption plan. The things of this world are only temporary and of no real value when you leave this place, but what Jesus has for you will last throughout all eternity. 1 John 1:6 says, *"If we say that we have fellowship with him, and walk in darkness, we lie, and do not the truth."* Jesus said if we want to get it right, we've got to repent. This does not mean we just go through the motions, but it actually means that we turn away from those things that have separated us from the Lord and enter into a full-time relationship with Him. This will require us to be real in our decision and our actions.

The Promise (verse 20-21)

I think I need to remind us all that with Jesus, there is an upside! He's a savior that has it all in one bag, knows what's going on, and can fix whatever might be broken. Everywhere in the Scriptures we're told that if we meet the conditions of God, we can anticipate the blessings of God. There is no difference here. Notice the conditions; Jesus said *"behold, I stand at the door and knock: if any man hear my voice, and open the door, I will come in to him, and will sup with him, and he with me."* A close examination of this text tells us that Jesus is standing at the ready to provide salvation, healing, deliverance, protection, peace, etc. with anyone who wants it, but they have to open the door to get it. We've been opening the wrong doors in this life! We've opened the doors of worldly opportunity, but not the door of surrendering all to Jesus; we've opened the doors of worldly knowledge, but not the door of the truth of the word of God; we've opened the door of happiness, but have not even approached the door that opens up to joy! Jesus says here that if we would just open the door, He would come in to be with us, and we will be with Him. We've got to meet the conditions of the Lord.

He again talks about the overcomer. This is a statement He's made to each of the churches of Asia Minor. All of them have the capacity of becoming overcomers. It was possible then, and it's possible right now. Let me ask you a question.... Are you an overcomer? If you know Jesus and have accepted Him as Lord and savior, that makes you an overcomer! You have overcome sin through the power of Jesus; you have overcome the things of this world, through the power of Jesus. Jesus has a special promise for the overcomer and states that they will sit on His throne. One thing we can note of His throne is that it's an everlasting throne. Hebrews 1:8 says, *"But unto the Son he saith, Thy throne, O God, is for ever and ever: a scepter of righteousness is the scepter of thy kingdom."* You meet the condition, and you can anticipate an everlasting promise coming your way.

I'd like to submit to you that the Lord is not looking for a lukewarm church; nor a compromising church; nor a dying church. I believe the Lord will come back for a church without spot or wrinkle that He can present to Himself as a glorious church. I'm talking about a loving church; I'm talking about a church that has endured persecution; I'm talking about a faithful church. This is a church that knows and accepts Jesus as Lord.

So the question remains...**Which Church Are You?**

SUMMARY

We're living in a day and time whereby there is something different about the way we do "church" and it is my opinion that it's time for us to return to what our forefather's called, "the old landmark." It's time for us to get back to the basics and get away from religion as we understand it, and embrace a relationship with God, which is what He's wanted from the very beginning. It's time for us to develop a deeper understanding of the word of God; it's time for us to get back to acknowledging who Christ is, what He's already done, and what He's yet going to do in the future.

The seven churches of Asia Minor in the Book of Revelation had their struggles, challenges, and obstacles, but one thing they all had in common was the fact that they were all churches of Jesus Christ!

Each church had its share of ups and downs, and if we're real with ourselves, we can see some of the same things happening today that was taking place according to the Scriptures.

The church today should not be surprised by the events happening before our very eyes as the Word of God foretold those events to take place in the last days. Everything up to now is pointing to the imminent return of Jesus Christ when He comes to rapture (snatch away) His church from the earth, which is the next event on God's prophetic time line. When He comes, we must be ready to answer the question... **Which Church Are You?**

BIBLIOGRAPHY

Amplified Bible, © 1965, Zondervan Publishing House, Grand Rapids, MI

Barnes, Albert, "Barnes' Notes of the New Testament," Baker House Books, Grand Rapids, MI

Dake, Finis J, "Dake's Annotated Reference Bible," Dake Bible Sales, Inc., Lawrenceville, GA

Hughes, Barbara, "Disciplines of a Godly Woman," Crossway Books, Wheaton, IL

McGee, Dr. J. Vernon, "Thru The Bible," Volume V, Thomas Nelson Publishers, Nashville, TN

Preacher's Outline and Sermon Bible, Revelation, New Testament, Volume 13, Leadership Ministries Worldwide, Chattanooga, TN

Strong, Edward, "Strong's Exhaustive Concordance of the Bible," Updated Edition, Hendrickson Publishers

OTHER WORKS BY DR. PERKINS

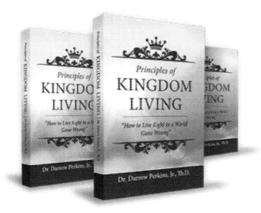

Using the Sermon on the Mount as a foundational background. This book deals with the issues that all of us go through as human beings. Living in a world that has basically turned it's back on doing things "decently and in order," this book gives practical guidance to handling today's situations, from discouragement (Poor in spirit) to death (Mourning) and all points in between. In this book, you will find information on: Church Membership; Divorce; Forgiveness; Prayer; and Trusting God.

This book can be ordered at **www.darrowperkinsjr.com**.

Printed in the United States
By Bookmasters